Prof. Wu Zuoren, Honorary President of the Central Academy and famous artist, drew the frontispiece, The Giant Panda.

Prof. Chen Shuliang, Vice-President of the Central Institute of Arts and Crafts, and famous calligrapher, wrote the Chinese title of this book.

大熊貓

THE GIANT PANDA

Editors
Zhu Jing and Li Yangwen

SCIENCE PRESS

Beijing, China 1980

Distributed by Van Nostrand Reinhold Company

New York   Cincinnati   Toronto   London   Melbourne

Copyright © 1980 by Litton Educational Publishing, Inc.

The Copyright is owned by Science Press and Litton Educational Publishing, Inc.

Published by Science Press, Beijing

Distributed by Van Nostrand Reinhold Company

New York, Cincinnati, Toronto, London, Melbourne

Printed by C & C Joint Printing Co., (H.K.) Ltd.

First published 1981

ISBN 0-442-20064-1

Science Press Book No. 1993-3

EDITORS

Zhu Jing, Li Yangwen

CONTRIBUTORS

Li Yangwen, Liao Guoxin, Li Shuzhong, Chen Daizong
Jiang Shaozhong, Ye Juqun, Liu Weixin, Li Chengzhong
(Beijing Zoo)

Zhu Jing, Long Zhi
(Institute of Zoology, Academia Sinica)

He Donghai, Pan Huigen
(Shanghai Science and Educational Film Studio)

Pu Tao
(Wolong Natural Reserve, Sichuan Province)

Two of the photographs in the album are by courtesy of Lu Changkum, formerly research fellow at the Institute of Zoology, Academia Sinica.
Translated by Fu Chue and Chang Lunghsi

PREFACE

The giant panda (*Ailuropoda melanoleuca*) is a world-famous precious animal exclusively indigenous to China, and also a favourite with peoples of all countries for the unusual and beautiful colouring of its fur, its unique features, its easy and graceful manner, and its gentle disposition and amusing behaviour. It has become very well-known as a messenger of friendship sent by the people of China to the rest of the world. By using the giant panda as its emblem, the World Wildlife Fund, an international organization for the conservation of rare and precious wildlife, has emphasized the value of this animal and that of other rare species as well as the importance of their conservation.

In systematics, the giant panda belongs to the Carnivora together with the wolf, bear, tiger, leopard, etc., but it is the only species that has changed from a carnivorous animal to one that lives on herbage. Some of its organs have consequently changed as a result of their adaptation to the new food, and the new characteristics developed from this adaptation have made its feeding habit even more particular. This complete departure from meat-eating has earned it the name of "monk among carnivores"*. Occasionally the giant panda shows a retrogression to its earlier instinct by preying on other animals. In view of its special characteristics, scholars have been unable to agree as to its right place in the history of evolution. Some scientists hold that it should come under the bear family; others classify it as a member of the procyon; while still others put it in a separate family. On the basis of results from recent investigation, Chinese zoologists maintain that the giant panda should be classified as belonging to a distinct taxonomic family—Ailuropodidae. Even the Chinese name for the panda, "xiong-mao" or bear-cat, is controversial, as the panda is neither a

---

* A Buddhist monk abstains from eating meat.

bear nor a cat, neither a bear-like cat nor a cat-like bear. The two words of the compound name, therefore, should not be construed as modifying each other, but rather simply as the entity of a term denoting a species—the panda.

In the evolution of the carnivores, the giant panda differentiated rather early to form a separate branch, thriving and flourishing during a geologic period some hundred thousand years ago. Information gathered by our palaeontologists during years of excavation shows that the giant panda had a very wide distribution at that time in most of the regions in eastern China. Its remains have been found even outside China, in the northern part of Burma. Such wide distribution has entitled it to be a typical species, a representative of the fauna in south China in the mid-Pleistocene epoch, known as the panda-stegodon fauna, of which it is the only survival today. Having gone through a long period of evolution, the panda nevertheless retains many of its primitive features so that it can be regarded as an "old-timer" and a "living fossil". The range of its distribution, however, has been drastically reduced. According to the investigation of recent years, Chinese zoologists have charted its distribution within a limited area of the southern range of the Qin Ling Mountains in Shaanxi, the Min Mountains bordering south Gansu and running into Sichuan Province, and the Qionglai and Balang Mountains, the Great and the Lesser Xiang Hills and Liang Mountains in Sichuan.

Many factors have conspired to reduce gradually the number of pandas in the wild. The encroachment of human activities in particular has greatly damaged the environment of the panda's former habitat and has thus reduced its range. Moreover, the slowness of development of panda babies, their late maturity and high selectivity in mating, the small number of the young born in a litter, the helplessness and vulnerability of their cubs, their low survival rate and long reproduction cycle—all these intrinsic factors tend to endanger their propagation and to reduce them to such a rarity that the Chinese government has found it necessary to set up natural reserves and to take various measures for their conservation and that of other wildlife.

Quite a number of carnivores live separately because they are at the pyramidal top of the food web in nature and their food supplies of their choice are both limited and hard to obtain; whereas most herbivores live in herds. The panda, though living mainly on plants such as the arrow-bamboo, has maintained its solitary habits and is called the "hermit of the bamboo forests". It does not migrate in summer or winter, but lives rather permanent in a place. The mating season is spring and it then roams far and wide in search for a mating partner.

With rather childlike simplicity, the panda is not only graceful and charming in manner but is also of great value to science. Many questions concerning this animal have aroused much interest among scientists and given rise to in-depth studies, a quite important one of these is the problem of preserving the species by breeding the animal in captivity. Since the exhibition of giant pandas in Chinese zoos in 1953, we have solved many problems regarding their keeping and breeding in captivity. In 1963, the female panda Li Li and male panda Pi Pi in the Beijing Zoo mated, and gave birth to Ming Ming on September 9th of the same year. This is the world's first successful breeding of the giant panda in captivity. Since then several litters have been born under the same conditions. In 1978 the Beijing Zoo made the first successful experiment in artificial insemination with the giant panda, and a cub named Yuanjing was born. This has opened up new breeding possibilities. Li Li, the female who was the first to give birth to a cub in the Beijing Zoo, and who has lived there for 23 years, is the panda that has lived the longest in captivity and is still going strong at the moment.

The giant panda enjoys great popularity throughout the world, but most of us have to be content to see it in the zoo, for the panda lives in the secret recesses of dense forests in high mountains that even in China few have the chance and luck to see it in nature. The pandas one sees in the zoo are mostly adults. Under these conditions it is almost impossible, even though very desirable, to enjoy the sight of charming and mischievous baby pandas, and to observe their growth and development. It is hoped that this album will provide the readers through numerous photographs, with some first-hand information about the habitat, food supplies, and behaviour of the giant panda in the wild, and about the growth of its cubs in captivity, so that they may know more about this rare animal.

The photographs published here have been taken in the course of investigation as data for research. They represent in four parts: ecology, growth and conservation of the giant panda itself and its mission as a messenger of friendship. We would like to acknowledge that we are specially indebted to Professor Wu Zuoren, famous artist, Honourary President of the Central Academy of Arts, for his painting of the giant panda as a special contribution to this album and to Professor Chen Shulang, famous calligrapher, Vice-president of the Central Institute of Arts and Crafts for his handwriting of an inscription of the title of this book. Heartfelt thanks are also due to our friends for all the support and encouragement we have received from them in the compiling of this book. We are also greatly indebted to the Science Press and to our colleagues Zhang Zhiqiang and Chen Wenjian for their assistance in the preparation of this album. We hope that this album would reflect the biological characteristics of the giant panda in nature and in captivity, and thus be of great interest both to the professional and to the amateur. As all the photographs were taken at first hand as data for research, they are bound to be affected by the limitations of our working conditions as well as by our individual taste. Any suggestion or advice from our readers will be much appreciated.

Zhu Jing   Li Yangwen
July 1980

CONTENTS

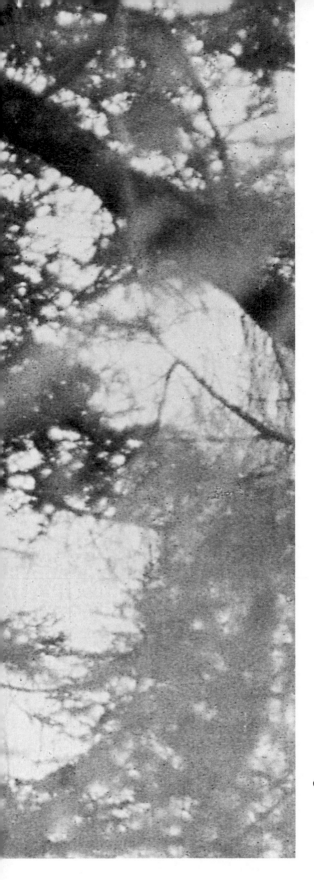

Giant panda.

Li Li cuddling Ming Ming. The first successful birth in captivity
—September 9th, 1963.

Li Li after 23 years in Beijing Zoo. About 5 years old when caught in 1957.

Ming Ming now in Changsha Zoo.

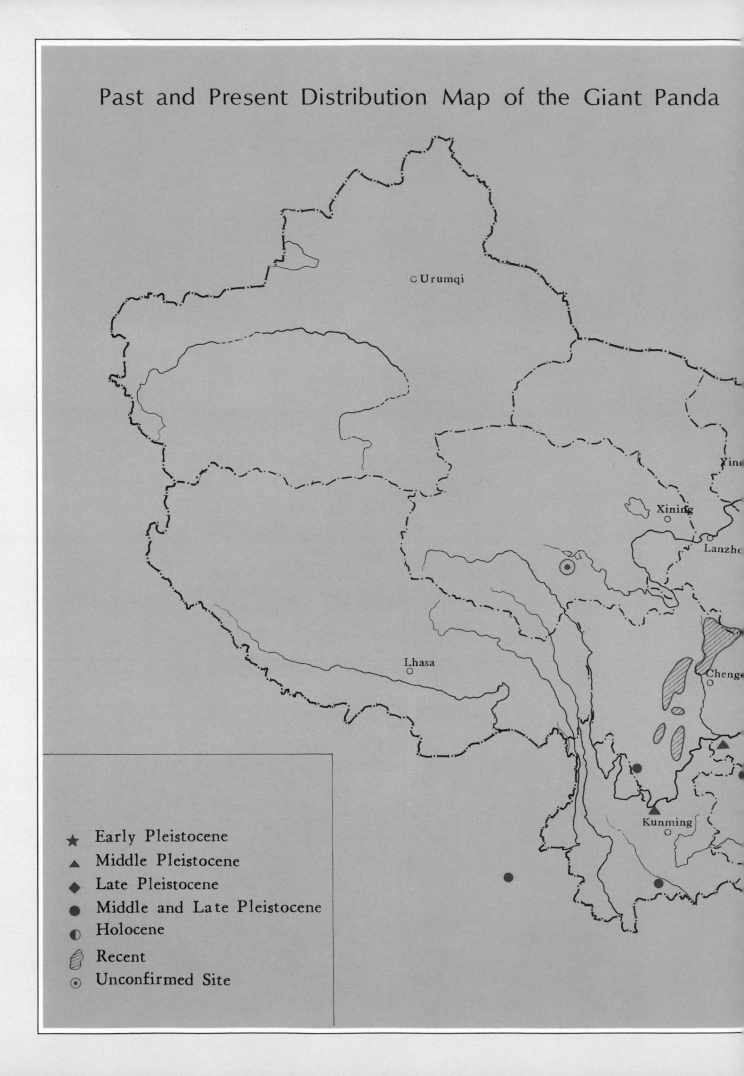

Past and Present Distribution Map of the Giant Panda

Urumqi

Yin

Xining

Lanzho

Lhasa

Cheng

Kunming

★ Early Pleistocene
▲ Middle Pleistocene
◆ Late Pleistocene
● Middle and Late Pleistocene
◑ Holocene
🖋 Recent
⊙ Unconfirmed Site

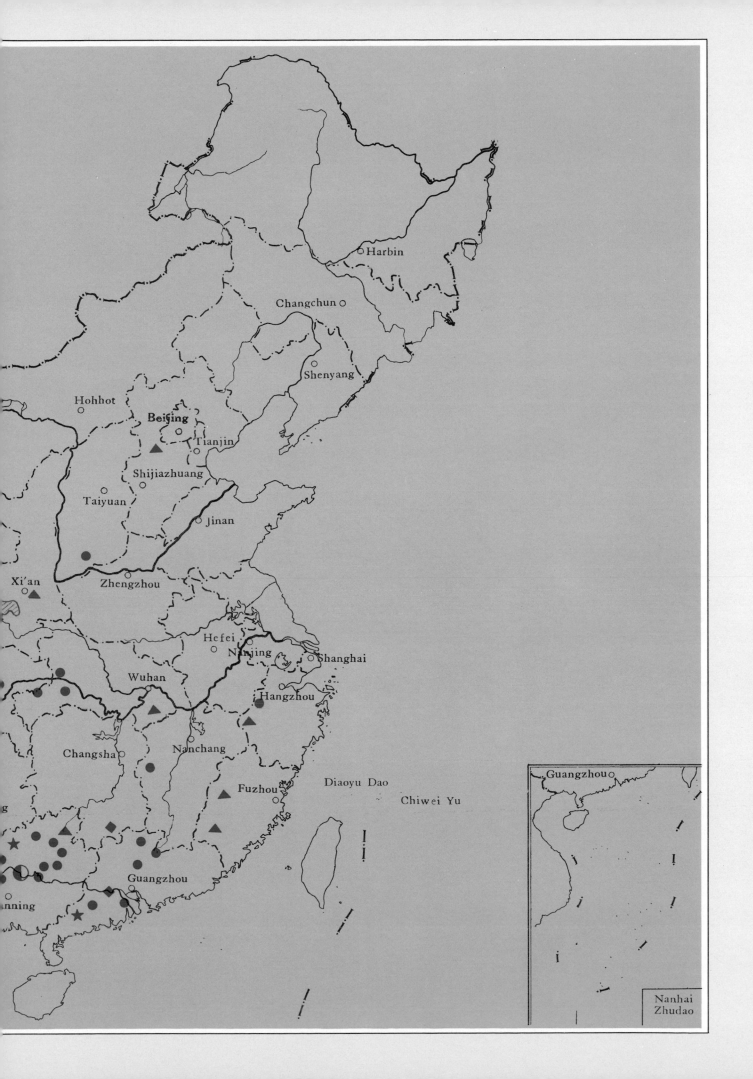

Harbin

Changchun

Shenyang

Hohhot

Beijing

Tianjin

Shijiazhuang

Taiyuan

Jinan

Xi'an

Zhengzhou

Hefei

Nanjing

Shanghai

Wuhan

Hangzhou

Changsha

Nanchang

Fuzhou

Diaoyu Dao

Chiwei Yu

Guangzhou

nning

Guangzhou

Nanhai
Zhudao

Distribution, Habitat and the Bamboo Jungle

Enjoys to see endless mountains wrapped up in snow.
Qionglai mountains (left). Balang mountains (right)—the main montane, region where
the giant panda lives.

Countless verdured mountains.

Min mountains—another main montane, region where the giant panda lives.

Country of the panda—a landscape of its habitat.

Alpine meadow, 3800 metres above sea level.

Altitudinal belts of the vegetation in the distribution area.

The *Meconopsis*.

Alpine shrub-land, 3500-3300 metres above sea level.

Subalpine coniferous forest belt, 3500-2400 metres above sea level—panda's main habitat. Fir, spruce—arrow-bamboo forest.

Alpine lake—the Changhai in Jiuzhaigou, Nanping. 3000 metres above sea level.

Lake at the lower limit of the coniferous forest belt.

Summer on the fringe of fir, spruce—arrow-bamboo forests in the forest.

Spring in the fir, spruce—arrow-bamboo forests.

Early winter.

Fir, spruce——arrow-bamboo forests.

Late autumn.

A giant panda in the vast expanse of snow. 2800 metres above sea level. The giant panda does not hibernate or migrate in winter.

Autumn.   Spruce—birch, poplar, maple—arrow-bamboo forest.

Coniferous and deciduous mixed forest, 2500 (or 2400)—2000 metres above sea level——another habitat of the panda.

A lake in the mixed coniferous and deciduous forest.

Long for country.

Typical landscape of panda's habitat—gentle slope of the mountain ridges (near to the watershed, 3000-2400 metres above sea level).

Different types of
biotope in the
panda's habitat.

Sunny slope.   Deforested land.
Arrow-bamboo jungle.

Sunny slope.   Conifer—arrow-bamboo
jungle.   Fringe of the forest.

Sparsely-wooded conifer—bamboo
forest on the sunny slope.

Coniferous and deciduous mixed forest
with bamboo groves on the shady slope.

Conifer forest with bamboo groves
on the shady slope.

Bamboo jungle (maximum density of about
120-130 bamboos, with culms of 8-12 mm
in diameter per square metre).

Major species of arrow-bamboo, panda's main food.

Arrow-bamboo jungle in the forest about 40-80 bamboos with culms of 8-12 mm in diameter per square metre.

Fargesia spathacea, 3300-2000 metres above sea level.

Sinarundinaria chungii, 2400-1400 metres above sea level.

Activities of the Giant Panda

"A gap! Let's get in and track the panda!" Traces of the panda can be seen only in the recesses of bamboo jungle.

Panda's trail in bamboo jungle.

Dense bamboo jungle forming a tunnel-like covering.

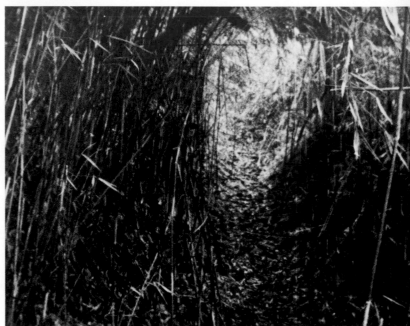

Traces of panda's feeding activities along both sides of
the path. The panda is in the habit of lingering for
food while waddling along.

Remains of feeding and panda's droppings.

Giant panda——hermit of the bamboo jungle.

Look! It's sitting right there!

We're discovered!

Self-assured panda ignores spectators.

Oh! What a reward at last! A panda
pops out its head from the bamboo
grove.

Look how the panda grasps the bamboo—by using the claws of its forepaw and the pseudo-thumb known as the radial sesamoid or the sixth claw.

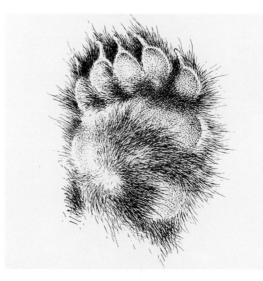

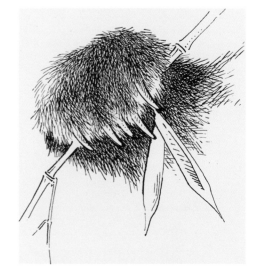

Grasping bamboo in both paws.

Droppings——the best clue for tracking panda. They serve as the best sign of its whereabout time of activity and direction of movement.

Heaps of dung. The droppings are relatively large: 6-9 cm in diameter and 12-20 cm long. The panda has evolved from a carnivorous animal to a herbivorous one. It has, however, its fibre-digesting ability though it is not as great as that of cows and sheep. There are a lot of undigested bamboo leaves and fibres in its droppings.

New droppings, moist with mucous on the surface, smelling of green bamboo.

Mouldy, old droppings on wet soil.

Old droppings on dry land, dark brown in colour.

Droppings after eating bamboo shoots.
Pandas like to eat arrow-bamboo
shoots in summer.

Arrow-bamboo jungles provide the animal not only
with food but also secluded habitat.

A lair among bushes.

A lair in dense bamboo groves.

Pandas seldom climb trees, still less sleep in trees.

46   A lair in arrow-bamboo groves.

A tree hole 2800 metres above sea level in which a litter of panda cubs were born here in the autumn of 1977.

Look! The fur of this baby panda born in the wild looks thicker and longer than those of cubs born in captivity.

Panda's main diet is arrow-bamboo, but it also
eats more than twenty other kinds of food.

Trail for seeking food among *Equisetum*.

Remains after a meal of scouring rush
(*Equisetum*).

Droppings after a meal of *Equisetum*.

Droppings after eating *Aster*.

It also eats meat!

Claw marks left on the poplar (*Populus*).

Peeling the bark of *Salix* for food.

Claw marks left on Abies.

Peeling the bark of *Salix* for food.

Panda's activities in nature for one day,
its entire life in miniature.

Gazing into the distance.

Wanting to have a
try at climbing.

Unable to climb,
just wade across.

Pandas do not usually climb trees. Generally they climb trees only in an emergency.

Natural Regeneration of Bamboo Plants and the Vicissitudes of the Giant Panda

The law of nature——succession of vegetation. Regeneration of arrow-bamboo groves. The cycles of blossoming and seed bearing of various species are different, but all subject to the influence of environment.

A rare sight a century. Arrow-bamboo blossoming over large tracts of land in the Min Mountains and its subsequent withering (1975-1976).

Blossoms of *Sinarundinaria chungii.*

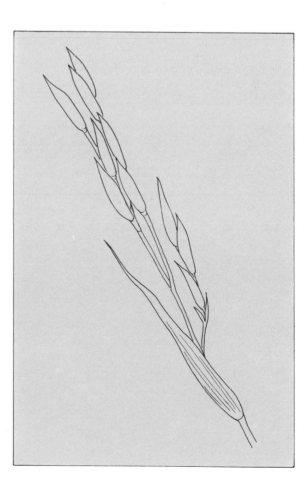

Blossoms of *Fargesia spathacea*.

Withered bamboo and mouldy roots, that can grow no more shoots.

Regeneration. Young bamboos newly grown.
Seedlings of *Fargesia spathacea*.

Stretches of young bamboo.

Bamboo seedlings grow steadily but very slow. Plants of arrow-bamboo all still too young to be food for the panda.

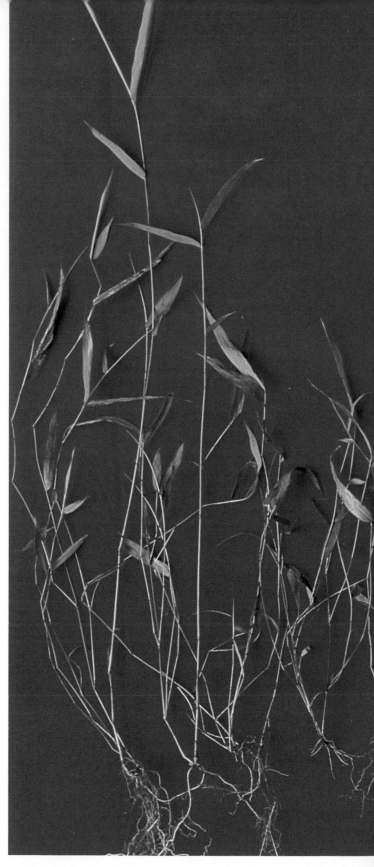

Young bamboo of 1-4 years. Arrow-bamboo seedlings will grow from seeds fallen the plant to the ground, though it takes one to two years to germinate. The seedlings grow new roots and new shoots every year. They grow gradually. It generally takes 14-15 years for the bamboo to grow to more than 7-8 mm in diameter and about 3 metres in height. They will form a forest, only then can they become a source of food and a home for the panda.

Arrow-bamboo withered after blossoming. Famine appeared——
the danger of death. Some pandas moved out of the disaster area,
some were caught by it there.

Withered bamboo.

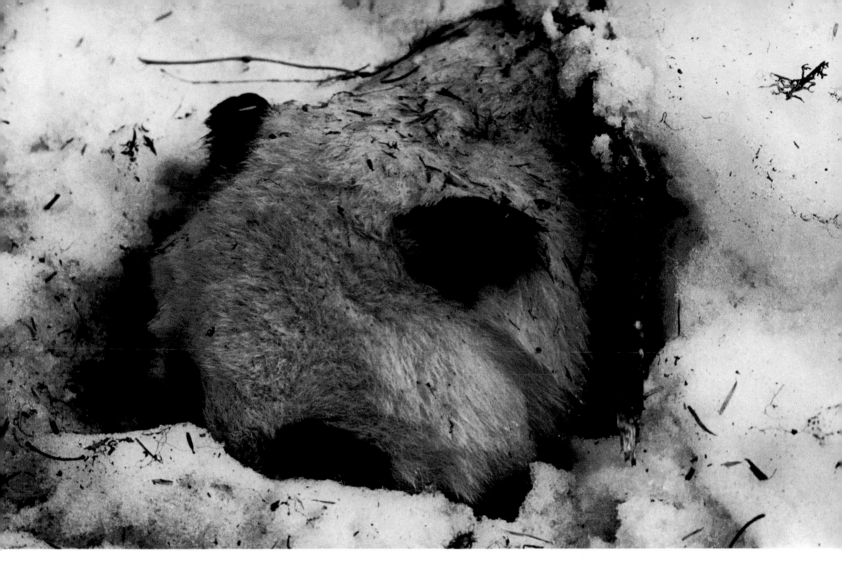

Eternal rest under the snow.

Skeleton.

Birth, old age, sickness and death——the law of nature,
which even the precious giant panda cannot escape.

Sign of malnutrition—ascites.

Weakening of viscera.

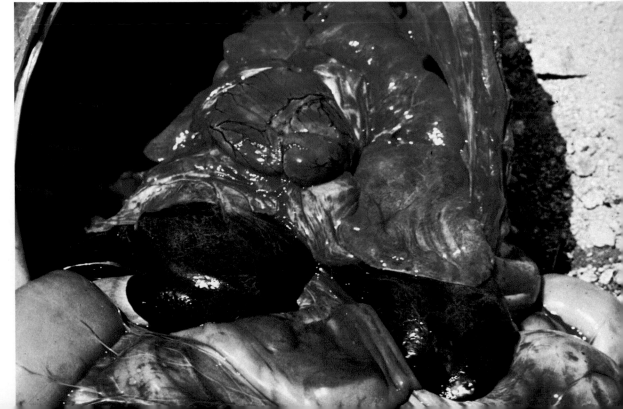

66

Round worm—a common parasite of the giant panda.

A carcass in withered bamboo groves.

Frozen carcass in forest snow—end of suffering from hunger and cold.

Died of starvation—in a famine-stricken area.

Of course, there are other reasons.

How many such changes have appeared in the history of the earth——evolution.

The giant panda survives in all its dignity.

Reproduction

The vigour of life—reproduction of species.

Mating (a copulating posture).

Mating (after ejaculating).

74

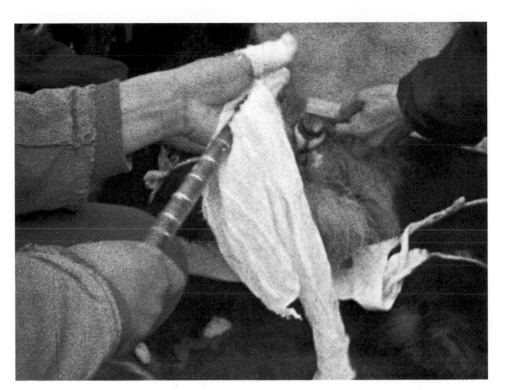

External genitals of male panda. Artificial collection of semen.

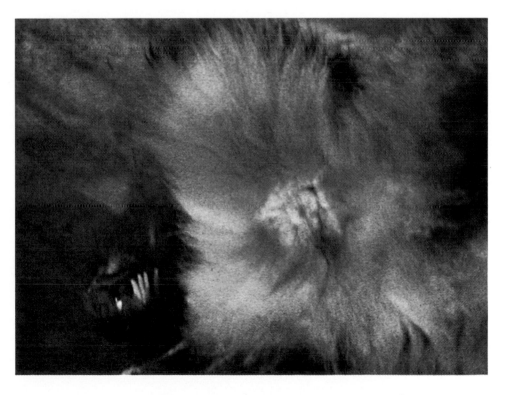

Characteristics of the external genitals of female panda in oestrus.

Huan Huan is rubbing its genitals when in heat.

Sperm of the panda.

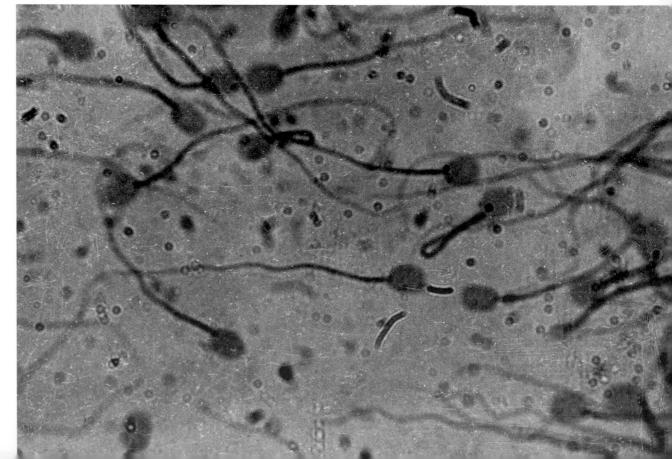

Mother panda sound asleep after giving birth.

Growth of Panda Cubs

New life. Birth of a baby panda. Panda cubs weigh only 90-130g at birth and are 15-17 cm long. They are wholly white with little fur. The head is more flat and rotund than that of the adult. Though tiny at birth, it has a loud call which will later become low-pitched.

The adult panda has a very short tail while that of the young cub is about 1/3-1/5 of its total body length. The latter will decrease in proportion to the panda's growth.

Change of appearance.   Black fur begins to grow on the ears, eyes and shoulders a week after birth.   After 10 days, more dark patches appear on the fore limbs and hind limbs, then begin to spread gradually as their colour becomes darker and darker.   The eye patches are at first round like a pair of sun-glasses, making the cub look comical.   After about half a month, the patches become oblong thus setting the face pattern of a giant panda.

Look at my face, eyes shut—expressionless.

Mother panda picks up her cub.

First try.

Another try.

Carrying the cub in the mouth..

Protecting the cub.

Bringing it near the mouth.

Lowering it again. Doesn't know how to fondle it.

A month cub.

Yuanjing a month old—the first birth given by the giant panda by successful artificial insemination. Born on September, 8th 1978.

One-month-old cub, black and white, typical face pattern, panda-like in appearance, tail still a bit too long, limbs still too weak to stand. Cannot move about, but only sleep and suckle. Will crawl on mother's breast seeking milk when hungry. Often rolls over on its side. Eyes not yet open, but sensitive to light; they will be half-open after 40 days.

Mother panda protecting its baby.

It becomes a little difficult for the mother panda to pick up her month-old cub; she uses both mouth and paws.

Final success!

Sleeping cub with sleepy mother.

Two months old. 3-4 kg in weight. Now, it can move about and crawl a little. Its four limbs cannot move in coordination yet. Just opened its eyes, but sight and reflex instinct still rather poor.

Two months old.

Holding the cub in its arms.

98

Struggling to be free. Although it cannot walk, it can turn and toss in mother's arms.

Suckling.

Suckling while lying on its back. New born cub suckles 6-12 times every 24 hours, for 15-30 minutes each time. The mother sits holding the cub in her arms, while the cub lies on stomach to suckle. When one breast is exhausted, the mother will move the cub to the other with her forepaws, while using her nozzle to help in the transfer. The number of sucklings will be reduced to 3-4 times a day after two months; and then 2-3 times a day after 3-4 months, by which time the cub will have learned to suckle while sitting or lying on its back.

Three months old. The cub is now about 5 kg in weight, with a pair of clear bright eyes. It can stand on its own legs and make a few steps. It likes to move about and often rolls over on its side. Teeth begin to cut. All the milk teeth will have cut within a year.

Three months old.

Maternal love.

Cuddling and teasing.

A kiss between mother and daughter.

Ashamed.

Four months old.

Four months old. Weighs 8-9 kg but its limbs are still rather weak. Likes to walk around, can run for a short distance and loves to play and roll on the ground. It is quite clumsy in its movements. It won't wander far from its mother.

Look! Toss it up, hold it in her arms again.

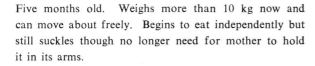

Five months old.

Five months old. Weighs more than 10 kg now and can move about freely. Begins to eat independently but still suckles though no longer need for mother to hold it in its arms.

Doing exercises. Look! It wants to climb on
mother's back to play.

Six months old.

Six months old. 12-13 kg in weight, can be weaned now, but still cannot leave its mother.

It's becoming more and more difficult for the mother panda to hold it.

Still wants to hold it in its arms even though hardly possible.

Struggling in vain to get loose.

Seven months old.

Longing for the wild.

Yearning for maternal love.

The naughty baby. "It's my turn to play with you now." Roles have changed.

Look! It wants to climb on top of mother's back.

The Giant Panda in the Zoo

Looking at the world.

Holding its food.

Still shy.

Entering a wider world for the first time.

Eight months old. Climbing.

Eight months old.

Playing with a ball.

Nine and a half months old.

Facing the wall.

"Look! I'm ten months old."

Ten months old.

Eleven months old.

One year old.

One year old. Celebrating its birthday. A dignified giant panda.

13 months old.

13 months old. Still a young panda cub, climbing and riding.

14 months old.

14 months old. Comfortable and happy.

15 months old.

15 months old. Can adapt in captivity to a bamboo diet.

144

16 months old.

16 months old. Facing the rock, hoping to climb.

17 months old. Being leisurely and carefree.

17 months old.

18 months old. Roaming in its garden.

18 months old.

19 months old.

19 months old. Fond of green bamboo for food.

Buried in thought.

Living in the Panda House in the Beijing Zoo.

148

Enjoying a happy life.

In unity is strength.

Thriving and prosperous.

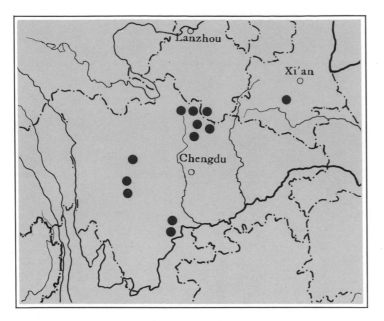

Distribution map of reserves for the giant panda.

Conservation

All the world know.

Sending the panda to its homeland.

Messenger of Friendship

Messenger of friendship. Leaving native country, reluctantly parting.

Friendship between China and Korea—Dan Dan.

Giant panda in Washington.

Close neighbours separated only by a strip of water—Friendship between China and Japan—Kang Kang.

The Panda House in the Ueno Zoo.

Huan Huan—sowing the seed of friendship.

Ching Ching and Chia Chia in the London Zoo.

Ching Ching and Chia Chia are playing with water.

LA REPUBLICA POPULAR DE CHINA, EN NOBLE GESTO DE AMISTAD, DONO AL PUEBLO MEXICANO LOS DOS EJEMPLARES DE OSOS PANDA QUE AQUI SE EXHIBEN.

ES UN PRIVILEGIO PARA EL ZOOLOGICO DE LA CIUDAD DE MEXICO CONTAR CON TAN BELLOS Y EXCEPCIONALES ESPECIMENES.

11 DE SEPTIEMBRE DE 1975

Ying Ying and Pe Pe in the city of Mexico for friendship between the peoples of China and Mexico.

Sowing the seed of friendship in the Madrid Zoo.

For Sino-French Friendship—Panda in Paris.

CHRONICLE OF EVENTS ABOUT THE GIANT PANDA

The giant panda, recorded as a rare and valuable animal in ancient Chinese classics and local chronicle, was not introduced into modern science, nor known by the general public until 1869. A brief chronicle events of its later history is given in the following:

1869 11th Mar. The French missionary Père David discovered the giant panda in Baoxing Xian of Sichuan Province, China, with the help of the local people. He bought a giant panda's skin. Mar. 21st, sent panda's skin to Paris with a brief description which he requested to be published. It was published in the journal of the Paris Natural History Museum—*Voyage en Chine,* Nouv. Arch. Mus. Hist. Nat. Paris, 5 (Bulletin) pp. 3-13. The animal was named *Ursus melanoleucus.* Mar. 23rd, Père David obtained another corpse of young giant panda. Apr. 1st, obtained the body of an adult giant panda. This is the first time the giant panda was introduced into modern science.

1870 Alphonse Milne-Edwards decided that the giant panda was not a bear. Renamed it *Ailuropoda melanoleuca.*

1872 Père David published the first notes on the habits of the giant panda—Rapport adressé à MM. Les Professeurs—Administrateurs de Muséum D'Histoire Naturelle, Dec. 15th, 1871, Nouv. Arch. Mus. Hist. Nat. Paris, 7 (Bulletin), pp 75-100.

1874 Milne-Edwards published the first report on anatomy of the giant panda (1868-1874).

1915 A. S. Woodward published details of a fossil giant panda from Burma, *Aelureidopus baconi.*

1916 Hugo Weigold of the Stötzner Expedition acquired a living young giant panda which died shortly afterwards. The expedition collected a total of six skins.

1923 W. D. Matthew and W. Granger published details of a fossil giant panda from the Pliocene deposits of Yanjinggou in eastern Sichuan Province, and named it *Aeluropus fovealis.*

1929 13th Apr. During the Kelley—Roosevelt Expedition, Theodore and Kermit Roosevelt were the first to have shot an adult giant panda near Yuesi in the former Sikang Province. "Trailing the Giant Panda" was later published (1930).

1931 13th May Ernst Schaefer shot a young female giant panda on the Brooke Dolan Expedition.

1934 8th Dec. Dean Sage and William Sheldon shot an old female giant panda on the Dean Sage expedition.

1935 Apr. H. C. Brocklehurst shot a giant panda.

1936 9th Nov. Ruth Harkness organized an expedition, caught a living young giant panda in Zhaobaogou of Qionglai Mountains, Wenchuan Xian. The giant panda was called Su Lin and thought at the time to be a female though it was actually a male. Dec. 18th, Su Lin arrived in San Francisco. The first living giant panda exported from China. Dec. 23rd, Su Lin arrived in New York.

1937 8th Feb. Su Lin was deposited at Brookfield Zoo, Chicago, and became the first zoo-owned giant panda.

1937 Autumn, Ruth Harkness came to China and found two more young giant pandas, both believed to be females. She arranged to bring one back to the U. S. as mate for Su Lin.

1938 18th Feb. Ruth Harkness arrived at Brookfield Zoo with the second living panda. First named Diana, later renamed Mei Mei.

1938 Ruth Harkness published "The Lady and the Panda".

1938 1st Apr. Su Lin died from food obstruction in Brookfield Zoo. Ruth Harkness went to China on her third trip to find a mate for Mei Mei.

1938 10th June Roy Spooner brought a young female panda, Pandora, to New York Zoo (24 lb. in weight).

1938 24th Dec. Floyd Tangier Smith of England brought five giant pandas to London. A young female called Ming and four adults: Grumpy, Dopey, Happy and Grandma. Grumpy and Dopey, later renamed Tang and Sung, thought to be a male and a female. Happy was a male and Grandma an old female. Another panda (the sixth one) said to have died during the sea voyage. These are the first pandas to have arrived in England from their homeland China.

1939 26th Jan. Happy sold to Germany, toured German zoos for the first time. June 24th, Happy arrived at St. Louis Zoo which became its permanent home.

1939 1st May Male panda Pan arrived at New York Zoo as mate for Pandora.

1939 23rd May Sung transferred to Whipsnade Park.

1939 12th Sept. St. Louis Zoo acquired female panda Pao Pei as mate for Happy.

1939 16th Nov. Chicago Zoo acquired its third panda, male Mei Lan.

1941 30th Dec. John Tee-Van arrived at New York with Pandee and Pandah which were thought to be a pair. Presented to the U. S. United China Relief by Song Meiling.

1945 31st Dec. Lien Ho caught in Sichuan for London Zoo.

1946 30th Sept. Panda caught in Wenchuan Xian, Sichuan, for New York Zoo. Transported to Shanghai via Chengdu, died in Shanghai October 18th. Made into a specimen and deposited in Shanghai.

1946 26th Oct. Ta Kung Pao (Da Gong Bao) called out "Giant Panda is on the verge of extinction."

1947 14th May Ta Kung Pao reported that the painter Tang Youtang caught a male panda between the counties of Wenchuan and Mianzhu weighing 16 lb. Wanted to transport it to Shanghai for exhibition but failed.

1948 18th Dec. Dong Nan Ribao (Southeast Daily) reported a male panda was caught in Emei Mountain in mid-August, weighing 24 lb. Trained for four months for exhibition but project failed.

1953 Chengdu Zoo of Sichuan Province was keeping a giant panda. The first time a giant panda was exhibited in Chinese zoos. Panda lived three weeks in the zoo. It was only after liberation that Chinese zoo workers found themselves in a position to carry out researches on the life of rare animals and give them protection.

1955 June Beijing Zoo acquired three young pandas: Ping Ping (30 lb.), Hsing Hsing and Chi Chi I (both under 20 lb.). Ping Ping was a male while Hsing Hsing and Chi Chi I females.

1956 Beijing Zoo acquired another female panda Su Mao and in autumn, an unnamed male. The male died in Beijing Zoo December 31st.

1957 Beijing Zoo acquired female panda Li Li.

1957 18th May Beijing Zoo sent male panda Ping Ping to Moscow Zoo. This is the first panda to have arrived in the U.S.S.R.

1957 Dec. Six-month-old young female panda caught in Sichuan Province, named Chi Chi II.

1958 Jan. Chi Chi II arrived in Beijing.

1958 May Heini Demmer visited Beijing and chose Chi Chi II for exchange by an exchange negotiation. Brought Chi Chi II on a tour to Moscow, Berlin, Frankfurt and Copenhagen.

1958 5th Sept. Chi Chi II went to London for a three-week visit, sold to London Zoo September 26th.

1959 18th Aug. Male panda An An sent from Beijing to Moscow.

1959 Institutions of the Chinese government formulated regulation restricting exportation of rare and precious animals.

1960 Oct. Chi Chi II came into heat for the first time.

1961 Apr. Ivor Montagu visited Beijing Zoo. Five other giant pandas on exhibition in Chinese zoos at Shanghai, Nanjing, Kunming, etc.

1962 14th Sept. The State Council of China issued "Instructions on the active protection and rational utilization of wild animal resources," stipulating that the giant panda is a rare and precious animal protected by the government, and that natural reserves be established for its protection.

1963 9th Sept. Li Li mated with Pi Pi (male), gave birth to male Ming Ming. First successful breeding of giant panda in captivity.

1964 There were then three pandas in Shanghai Zoo, two in Guangdong, three in Chengdu and one in Harbin. Ming Ming was sent away from his mother.

1964 4th Sept. Li Li gave birth to female Lin Lin at Beijing, the second giant panda born in captivity, Chinese zoologists recorded accurate gestation period of giant panda: Ming Ming, 148 days; Lin Lin, 120 days, the latter gave premature birth to twin that did not live.   Giant panda's gestation period about 4-5 months.

1964 7th Dec.   D. Dwight Davis of the United States Published monograph on anatomy of the giant panda— *The Giant Panda, A Morphological Study of Evolutionary Mechanisms,* Fieldiana: Zool. Mem. 3 pp. 1-339.

1965 15th Feb.   Lin Lin separated from her mother Li Li.

1965   Four natural reserves established in Tianquan, Wenchuan, Pingwu and Nanping of Sichuan to protect the giant panda, takin, and golden monkey.

1965 3rd June   Beijing Zoo sent a pair of giant pandas to Pyongyang Zoo.

1965 Sept.   Caroline Jarvis, editor of the International Zoo Yearbook, visited Chinese zoos.   At the time, there were seven giant pandas in Beijing Zoo: Li Li, Pi Pi, Ming Ming, Lin Lin, a young adult female and a pair of wild cubs under one year old.   Shanghai Zoo had one young male and two adult females.   Nanjing had a female, Harbin a male, Hangzhou a female. Chengdu had three (sex unknown).   Number of pandas in Chongqing unknown.

1966 4th Feb.   Curator of Mammals of London Zoo visited Russia at invitation of Moscow Zoo to discuss possibilities of mating An An and Chi Chi II.   Moscow Zoo director, Igor Sosnovsky agreed to Chi Chi II's visiting An An in the spring.   If the mating were successful and there were any off-spring, they would belong to London Zoo.   Information obtained from Moscow Zoo indicated that An An had two periods of sexual excitement each year, a strong one from February to May, a weaker one in autumn.   It lost its appetite and had obvious testicular swellings when in heat.   Moscow Zoo giant panda Ping Ping was 144 kg in weight and was the heaviest specimen kept in zoos at the time.

1966 11th Mar.   Chi Chi II left London for Moscow on specially modified B.E.A.   Vanguard aircraft, accompanied by her head-keeper and London Zoo's senior veterinary officer.

1966 26th Mar.   Chi Chi II and An An met one another through wire partition.   They responded by bleating like sheep, showing much curiosity.   Chi Chi II and An An put together in same enclosure March 31st, but after circling and smelling one another they started to fight and had to be separated.

1966   "Men and Pandas" by Ramona and Desmond Morris published.

1967 Winter, 1968 Spring, 1969 Spring and Summer,   Under the auspices of the Chinese Ministry of Forestry, Chinese research institutes conducted a scientific survey of Wanglang Natural Reserve, Pingwu Xian, Sichuan.

1972 April   The people of China presented the people of the United States with two giant pandas. Washington Zoo director, Dr. T. Reed came to China first to gain experiences in panda's care. Chinese delegates Ding Hong, Ma Yong, etc. accompanied the pandas to Washington Zoo.

1972 28th Oct. The Chinese people presented the Japanese people with two pandas, Lan Lan (3 years old) and Kang Kang (2 years old), as messengers of friendship. The pandas from Beijing arrived at Ueno Zoo, Tokyo, Japan. Chinese delegates Zhang Xiaoguang, Du Hongzhang etc. accompanied the pandas to Japan.

1973 April Ueno Zoo of Japan sent three men to Beijing and Shanghai Zoos to gain experiences in panda's care.

1973 May *People's Pictorial* published "Information about Wanglang Natural Reserve", reporting protection of giant panda in Pingwu Xian, Sichuan.

China Reconstructs reported life, habits and distribution of giant panda in China.

1973 8th Dec. Yen Yen and Li Li arrived in Paris as the Chinese people's messengers, accompanied by Chinese delegates Li Changde, Shi Senming, etc.

1974 Summer, Researches made by Chinese zoologists on the giant panda published for the first time: management of panda in captivity, treatment of diseases, breeding in captivity, observations on growth and development of panda cubs, biological characteristics, systematic position and evolutionary history. The article appeared in "Acta Zoologica Sinica" Vol. 20, No. 2, edited by The Zoological Society of China and published by Science Press, Beijing.

1974 14th Sept. The Chinese people's messengers of friendship Ching Ching and Chia Chia arrived in England accompanied by Chinese delegates Du Hongzhang, Yang Chengfu, etc.

1975 10th Sept. Giant pandas Ying Ying and Pe Pe flew across the Pacific Ocean as Chinese people's messengers to Mexico for the first time. Escorted by Chinese delegates Yan Zhenhe, Zheng Zequan, etc.

1975 Oct. "The Giant Panda", a film, was produced by the Scientific Education Film, Shanghai.

1976 Vast stretches of arrow bamboo, main food of the panda in the region around Min Mountains, blossomed, grew seeds and withered.

1978 8th Sept. Beijing Zoo obtained first success in breeding giant panda by artificial insemination. Mother panda Juan Juan gave birth to Yuanjing. Semen came from male panda Lo Lo.

1978 25th Dec. Chinese people's friendly messengers Chiang Chiang and Shao Shao arrived at Madrid to sow the seed of friendship in a Mediterranean country. Escorted by Chinese delegates Ni Shufa, Ye Juqun, etc.

1980 29th Jan. Chinese people's friendly messenger Huan Huan left for Japan to become Kang Kang's partner. Escorted by Chinese delegates Li Changde, Xu Juanhua, etc.

1980 Dec. "Giant Panda" a pictorial record compiled jointly by the Institute of Zoology, Academia Sinica and the Beijing Zoo, putting together systematically for the first time the results of studies made by Chinese Zoologists. It is published by Science Press, Beijing at home and abroad in Chinese and English editions.

	Name	Sex	Date of capture	Persons involved	Zoo	Weight on arrival (kg)	Estima age c arriv (mont
1.	Su Lin	M	9 Nov., 1936	Mrs. Ruth Harkness	Chicago	6.35	
2.	Mei Mei (Diana)	M	1937	,,	,,	22.7	
3.	(unnamed)	F	1937	F. Tangier Smith			
4.	Pandora	F	1938	R. C. Spooner	New York	16	
5.	Ming	F	1938	F. Tangier Smith	London	25.4	
6.	Tang (Grumpy)	M	1938	,,	,,	68.1	
7.	Sung (Dopey)	M	1938	,,	,,	68.1	
8.	Grandma	F	1938	,,	,,	72.6	
9.	Happy	M	1938	,,	London St. Louis	108.96	
10.	(unnamed)		1938	,,			
11.	Pan	M	1939	Den Wei Han	New York	32.68	
12.	Pao Pei	F	1939	G. Campbell	New York	27.24	
13.	Mei Lan	M	1939	A. T. Steele	Chicago	29.5	
14.	Pandee	F	1941	J. Tee-Van	New York	28.6	
15.	Pandah	F	1941	,,	,,	25.87	
16.	Lien Ho	M	1945	Ma Tek	London	18.16	
17.	Ping Ping	M	1955	I. Sosnovsky	Moscow		24 mo
18.	Chi Chi	F	1957	H. Demmer	London	55.38	16 mo
19.	An An	M	1959	I. Sosnovsky	Moscow	104.87	24 mo
20.	(unnamed)			Ding Hong Li Yangwen	Pyongyang	108.96	60
21.	(unnamed)			,,	,,		60
22.	Lin Lin	M		Li Changde etc.	,,		36
23.	San Xing	F		,,	,,		36
24.	Ling Ling	F	1970	Ding Hong Ma Yong etc.	Washington	56.47	10
25.	Hsing Hsing	M	1971	,,	,,	27.73	12
26.	Lan Lan	F	1968	Zhang Xiaoguang Du Hongzhang	Tokyo	88.98	36
27.	Kang Kang	M	1970	,,	,,	60.38	24
28.	Yen Yen	F	1968	Li Changde Shi Senming	Paris	40	14
29.	Li Li	M	1972	,,	,,	20	13
30.	Ching Ching	F	1973	Du Hongzhang Yang Chengfu	London	51.2	24
31.	Chia Chia	M	1973	,,	,,	50.2	23
32.	Ying Ying	F	1974	Yen Zhenhe Zheng Zequen	Mexico	27	12
33.	Pe Pe	M	1974	,,	,,	22.75	11
34.	Chiang Chiang	M	1976	Ni Shufa Ye Juqun	Madrid	91.5	60
35.	Shao Shao	F	1975	,,	,,	71	36
36.	Dan Dan	M	1970		Pyongyang		
37.	Huan Huan	F	1975	Li Changde Xu Juanhua	Tokyo	95.5	96

FOREIGN ZOOS

ate of al at zoo	Date of death	Life span in zoo	Remarks
8, 1937	Apr. 1, 1938	14 months	first thought to be female
18, 1938	Aug. 3, 1942	4 yrs 6 months	first thought to be female
	1937		died on ship en route
10, 1938	May 13, 1941	2 yrs 11 months	
24, 1938	Dec. 26, 1944	6 years	
	Apr. 23, 1940	1 yr 4 months	
	Dec. 18, 1939	1 year	first thought to be female
	Jan. 9, 1939	1 month	
24, 1939	Mar. 10, 1946	6 yrs 9 months	sold to Germany on Jan. 26, 1939 for tour in Germany
	1938		died on ship en route
1, 1939	May 5, 1940	1 year	
12, 1939	June 24, 1952	12 yrs 9 months	
16, 1939	Sept. 5, 1953	13 yrs 10 months	
30, 1941	Oct. 4, 1945	3 yrs 9 months	first thought to be male
30, 1941	Oct. 31, 1951	9 yrs 10 months	
11, 1946	Feb. 22, 1950	3 yrs 9 months	first thought to be female
18, 1957	May 29, 1961	4 years	estimated to be 6 years 10 months old
26, 1958	July 22, 1972	13 yrs 10 months	estimated to be 15 years 4 months old
18, 1959	Oct. 18, 1972	13 yrs 2 months	estimated to be 15 years 2 months old
3, 1965	not known		
20, 1971			
,, 16, 1972			came into heat in 1979, mated but gave no birth
,, 28, 1972	Sept. 4, 1979		mated in 1979 conceived
,, 8, 1973	June 30, 1980		
,, 14, 1974	Apr. 20, 1974		died of pancreatitis
,, 10, 1975			
,, 25, 1978			
,, 20, 1979			
29, 1980